Can You Find?
An ABC Book
Parent's Introduction

We Both Read books have been developed by reading specialists to invite you and your child to interact together as each book is being read. This book is designed for a parent or adult to read the entire book to a child. However, your child is invited to actively participate by finding items in the pictures.

This book will help your child identify the letters in the alphabet and the sounds those letters make. You will read a short sentence with words that start with a particular letter of the alphabet, for example: "Alvin admires acting." As you read the sentence, it may be helpful to point to the beginning letter of each word and emphasize the sound that letter makes.

Then, you can invite your child to find things in the picture that start with the same beginning sound (alligator, apple, astronaut, etc.). You can help guide your child by pointing out something in the picture that starts with the sound of the letter and asking if he knows what it might be. If needed, you can say what it is, emphasizing the first sound in the word. On each page, you can also point to the two different ways that each letter can be written and invite your child to find those letters hidden in the picture.

Please note that for vowels *a, e, i, o,* and *u* the book only includes words and objects that start with the short vowel sound. This helps avoid confusion and emphasizes the vowel sound in words that your child will first begin to read. If you think your child is ready, you may want to explain that the vowels can also sometimes make the same sound as the letter name.

After you have gone through the book once, it may be fun and helpful to go through it again with your child. Remember to praise your child's efforts and keep the interaction fun. Try to keep these tips in mind, but don't worry about doing everything right. Simply sharing the book together will help prepare your child for reading and a lifetime of reading enjoyment!

Can You Find?

An ABC Book

A We Both Read® Book: Level PK–K
Guided Reading: Level AA

---

*Dedicated to Sarah Poindexter
with special thanks for her humor and joy over many years
teaching children about the letters of the alphabet*

Text Copyright © 2016 by Sindy McKay
Illustrations Copyright © 2016 by Matt Loveridge
Reading Consultant: Bruce Johnson, M.Ed.

We Both Read® is a trademark of Treasure Bay, Inc.

Published by Treasure Bay, Inc.
P.O. Box 119
Novato, CA 94948 USA

Printed in Malaysia

Library of Congress Catalog Card Number: 2015940397

ISBN: 978-1-60115-280-0

Visit us online at:
www.WeBothRead.com

PR-6-18

WE BOTH READ®

Can You Find?

An ABC Book

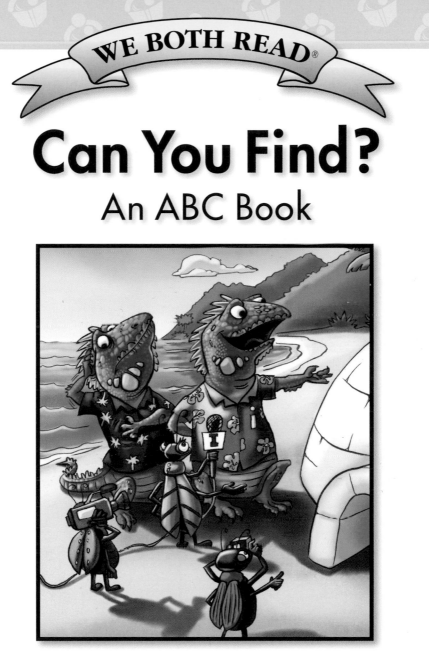

By Sindy McKay

Illustrated by Matt Loveridge

 TREASURE BAY

Alvin **a**dmires **a**cting.

Can you find some things in this picture that
have the same beginning sound as **Alvin**?

These words all start with the letter **A**.
The letter **A** can be written two ways:

A a

Can you find these letters hidden in the picture?

Bonnie **b**ursts **b**ubbles.

Can you find some things in this picture that
have the same beginning sound as **B**onnie?

These words all start with the letter **B**.
The letter **B** can be written two ways:

B b

Can you find these letters hidden in the picture?

Connor catches cows.

Can you find some things in this picture that have the same beginning sound as **Connor**?

6

These words all start with the letter **C**.
The letter **C** can be written two ways:

C c

Can you find these letters hidden in the picture?

David **d**irects **d**ucks.

Can you find some things in this picture that
have the same beginning sound as **D**avid?

These words all start with the letter **D**.
The letter **D** can be written two ways:

D d

Can you find these letters hidden in the picture?

Ellen **e**ducates **e**ggs.

Can you find some things that have the same beginning sound as **Ellen**? These words all start with the letter **E**. The letter **E** can be written two ways:

E e

Can you find these letters hidden in the picture?

Frank **f**umbles **f**ruit.

Can you find some things that have the same beginning sound as **Frank**? These words all start with the letter **F**. The letter **F** can be written two ways:

F f

Can you find these letters hidden in the picture?

Glenn **g**uards **g**eckos.

Can you find some things in this picture that start with the same beginning sound as **G**lenn?

These words all start with the letter **G**.
The letter **G** can be written two ways:

G g

Can you find these letters hidden in the picture?

<u>H</u>ank <u>h</u>andles <u>h</u>amburgers.

Can you find some things in this picture that
have the same beginning sound as **<u>H</u>ank**?

These words all start with the letter **H**.
The letter **H** can be written two ways:

H h

Can you find these letters hidden in the picture?

Ingrid interviews iguanas.

Can you find some things that have the same beginning sound as **Ingrid**? These words all start with the letter **I**. The letter **I** can be written two ways:

I i

Can you find these letters hidden in the picture?

<u>J</u>ack <u>j</u>umps over <u>j</u>elly <u>j</u>ars.

Can you find some things that start with the same beginning sound as **<u>J</u>ack**? These words all start with the letter **J**. The letter **J** can be written two ways:

J j

Can you find these letters hidden in the picture?

Karen **k**isses **k**oalas.

Can you find some things in this picture that start with the same beginning sound as **Karen**?

These words all start with the letter **K**.
The letter **K** can be written two ways:

K k

Can you find these letters hidden in the picture?

Laura licks lemons.

Can you find some things in this picture that
start with the same beginning sound as **Laura**?

These words all start with the letter **L**.
The letter **L** can be written two ways:

L l

Can you find these letters hidden in the picture?

Mikey makes music.

Can you find some things in this picture that
start with the same beginning sound as **Mikey**?

These words all start with the letter **M**.
The letter **M** can be written two ways:

M m

Can you find these letters hidden in the picture?

<u>N</u>ancy <u>n</u>eeds <u>n</u>apkins.

Can you find some things that have the same
beginning sound as **<u>Nancy</u>**? These words all start with
the letter **N**. The letter **N** can be written two ways:

N n

Can you find these letters hidden in the picture?

<u>O</u>scar <u>o</u>perates <u>o</u>ften.

Can you find some things that start with the same
beginning sound as **<u>O</u>scar**? These words all start with
the letter **O**. The letter **O** can be written two ways:

O o

Can you find these letters hidden in the picture?

Paul **p**roudly **p**lays **p**iano.

Can you find some things in this picture that start with the same beginning sound as **Paul**?

These words all start with the letter **P**.
The letter **P** can be written two ways:

P p

Can you find these letters hidden in the picture?

Quincy **q**uacks **q**uietly.

Can you find some things that have the same
beginning sound as **Quincy**? These words all start with
the letter **Q**. The letter **Q** can be written two ways:

Q q

Can you find these letters hidden in the picture?

<u>R</u>obin <u>r</u>ecognizes <u>r</u>ain.

Can you find some things that start with the same beginning sound as **<u>Robin</u>**? These words all start with the letter **R**. The letter **R** can be written two ways:

R r

Can you find these letters hidden in the picture?

<u>S</u>arah <u>s</u>leeps <u>s</u>oundly.

Can you find some things in this picture that start with the same beginning sound as **<u>S</u>arah**?

These words all start with the letter **S**.
The letter **S** can be written two ways:

S s

Can you find these letters hidden in the picture?

Tom **t**aps **t**errifically.

Can you find some things in this picture that start with the same beginning sound as **Tom**?

These words all start with the letter **T**.
The letter **T** can be written two ways:

T t

Can you find these letters hidden in the picture?

<u>U</u>ncle <u>U</u>nger <u>u</u>nloads <u>u</u>mbrellas.

Can you find some things that have the same
beginning sound as **<u>Uncle</u>**? These words all start with
the letter **U**. The letter **U** can be written two ways:

U u

Can you find these letters hidden in the picture?

<u>V</u>ictor <u>v</u>acuums <u>v</u>igorously!

Can you find some things that start with the same beginning sound as **<u>V</u>ictor**? These words all start with the letter **V**. The letter **V** can be written two ways:

V v

Can you find these letters hidden in the picture?

<u>W</u>alter <u>w</u>ashes <u>w</u>hales.

Can you find some things in this picture that have the same beginning sound as **Walter**?

These words all start with the letter **W**.
The letter **W** can be written two ways:

W w

Can you find these letters hidden in the picture?

Re**x** can fi**x** a Sphin**x**.

Can you find some things in this picture that _end_
with the same sound as **Rex**? These words _end_ with
the letter **X**. The letter **X** can be written two ways:

X x

Can you find these letters hidden in the picture?

<u>Y</u>ani <u>y</u>elped <u>y</u>esterday.

Can you find some things that have the same beginning sound as **<u>Y</u>ani**? These words all start with the letter **Y**. The letter **Y** can be written two ways:

Y y

Can you find these letters hidden in the picture?

<u>Z</u>elda <u>z</u>oomed <u>z</u>estfully.

Can you find some things that have the same
beginning sound as **<u>Z</u>elda**? These words all start with
the letter **Z**. The letter **Z** can be written two ways:

Z z

Can you find these letters hidden in the picture?

The Alphabet

Aa Bb Cc Dd

Ee Ff Gg Hh

Ii Jj Kk Ll

Mm Nn Oo Pp

Qq Rr Ss Tt

Uu Vv Ww Xx

Yy Zz

If you liked **Can You Find?**, here is another We Both Read® book you are sure to enjoy!

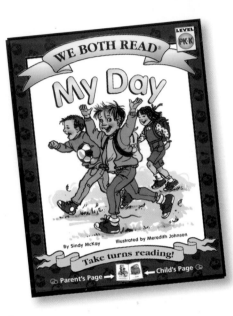

My Day

This book is designed for the child who is just being introduced to reading. The child's pages have only one or two words, which relate directly to the illustration and even rhyme with what has just been read to them. This title is a charming story about what a child does in the course of a simple happy day.

To see all the We Both Read books that are available,
just go online to **www.WeBothRead.com**.